LIGHTNING BOLT BOOKS™

Endangered and Extinct Mammals

Jennifer Boothroyd

Lerner Publications Company
Minneapolis

For Maddie
—J.B.

Lerner Publications Company
A division of Lerner Publishing Group, Inc.
241 First Avenue North
Minneapolis, MN 55401 U.S.A.

Website address: www.lernerbooks.com

Library of Congress Cataloging-in-Publication Data

Boothroyd, Jennifer, 1972–
        Endangered and extinct mammals / by Jennifer Boothroyd.
            pages   cm. — (Lightning bolt books™–Animals in danger)
        Includes index.
        ISBN 978-1-4677-1329-0 (lib. bdg. : alk. paper)
        ISBN 978-1-4677-2496-8 (eBook)
        1. Rare mammals—Juvenile literature. 2. Extinct mammals—Juvenile literature. 3. Endangered species—Juvenile literature. I. Title.
        QL706.8.B66 2014
        599.168—dc   232013013614

Manufactured in the United States of America
1 — PC — 12/31/13

Table of Contents

Mammals

Mammals are warm-blooded animals. Female mammals feed their young with milk.

Most mammals have fur or hair.

Mammals live all around the world. Some are in trouble. They are endangered.

Pandas are endangered. That means they are in danger of dying out.

Endangered Mammals

Asian elephants are some of the largest mammals on land. Their trunks are very strong.

Male elephants can weigh 11,900 pounds (5,400 kilograms).

Asian elephants are endangered.

Hunting endangered animals is against the law.

People used to hunt elephants for their tusks.

Long-nosed bats live in
Mexico. They are
in trouble.

Bats live in
caves in the
desert.

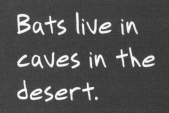

The bats have long tongues. They use them to eat nectar from flowers.

Bats look for food at night.

Endangered Ganges dolphins live in the rivers of India and Nepal.

This Ganges dolphin swims on its side. It drags a flipper to stir up small fish.

Ganges dolphins use their long beaks to find food at the bottom of the river.

African wild dogs have bushy tails. They have large ears.

These animals are in danger of dying out.

Animals in packs work together.

The wild dogs live in packs.
They hunt antelope and zebras.

This endangered pangolin lives on the Asian island of Java. It digs burrows underground.

This Malayan pangolin uses its long tongue to eat ants.

Most mammals have hair or fur.
Pangolins have scales.
People hunt them for their scales.

Pangolins roll up when in danger.

Extinct Mammals

Smilodons died out ten thousand years ago.

Some mammals have completely died out. **They are extinct.** Smilodons are an extinct mammal.

Smilodons are also called saber-toothed cats. **They had long, pointed teeth.**

Smilodons' two biggest teeth were 8 to 10 inches (20 to 25 centimeters) long.

The *Indricotherium* died out
25 million years ago.

These are the
largest land mammals
ever found.

Indricotherium were twice as tall as elephants.

Indricotherium were more than 18 feet (5.5 meters) tall.

Sea cows were more than 30 feet long (9 m). They weighed 22,000 pounds (9,980 kg).

Sea cows were huge water mammals.

Sea cows didn't have teeth.
They ate seaweed and kelp.

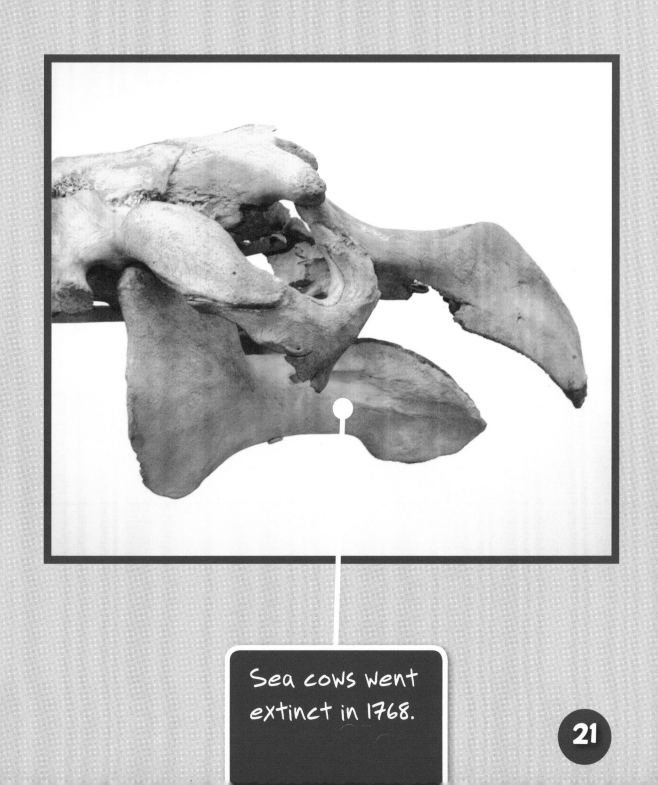

Sea cows went extinct in 1768.

Desert bandicoots lived in Australia. They ate insects and plants.

Desert bandicoots dug in the sand with their short front legs.

They disappeared more than fifty years ago.

Desert bandicoots are extinct.

Japanese river otters were covered with thick fur.

These otters had webbed feet. They hunted fish and shrimp.

The Japanese river otter was last seen in 1979. The otters were labeled extinct in 2012.

Many Japanese river otters died from hunting and pollution.

Helping Endangered Mammals

Mammals need healthy habitats to live. There are many ways people are saving endangered mammals.

People work to keep air, water, and land clean.

This area is a wildlife refuge. There are laws to protect this habitat and its animals.

People visit a wildlife refuge to learn about animals and plants that live there.

What you Can Do

There are many things you can do to help animals that are in danger.

- Pick up trash on the ground and in the water. Pollution can hurt animals.

- Plant a new tree or a bush in your yard.

- Recycle things to create less trash.

- Learn more about endangered animals.

- Visit zoos and other wildlife organizations. These places protect animals and their habitats.

A Remarkable Recovery

Only 136 grizzly bears lived in Yellowstone National Park in 1975. People were turning their habitat into ranches. Bears were hunted because they were killing farm animals. The US government created laws. The laws protected grizzly bears and their habitat. Many people worked to help the bears. These days, more than 600 bears are living in the area. National parks like Yellowstone protect endangered animals.

Glossary

burrow: an animal's underground shelter

endangered: at risk of dying out

extinct: died out

habitat: where an animal lives

law: a rule made by the government

mammal: a warm-blooded animal. Most have hair or fur. Female mammals make milk for their young.

pack: a group of animals that lives and hunts together

refuge: a place that gives protection to animals and plants

Further Reading

Hoare, Ben, and Tom Jackson. *Endangered Animals.* New York: DK Publishing, 2010.

Laverdunt, Damien. *Small and Tall Tales of Extinct Animals.* Wellington, NZ: Gecko Press, 2012.

Nature
http://www.pbs.org/wnet/nature/lessons/the-loneliest-animals/video-segments/4949

Neighborhood Explorers
http://www.fws.gov/neighborhoodexplorers

San Diego Zoo
http://kids.sandiegozoo.org/animals/mammals

Silverman, Buffy. *Do You Know about Mammals?* Minneapolis: Lerner Publications, 2010.

Index

Photo Acknowledgments

The images in this book are used with the permission of: © Japanese Museum of Nature and Science, p. 2; © Zuzana Buráňová/Dreamstime.com, p. 4; © Beer1970/Dreamstime. com, p. 5; © iStockphoto.com/ygluzberg, p. 6; © Jkfyates/Dreamstime.com, p. 7; © J. Scott Altenbach/Bat Conservation International, p. 8; © SearchNet Media/Flickr/ Getty Images, p. 9; © Roland Seitre/naturepl.com, p. 10; © 19th era/Alamy, p. 11; © iStockphoto.com/michael_price, p. 12; © Francois van Heerden/Shutterstock.com, p. 13; © Biosphoto/SuperStock, p. 14; AP Photo/Jefri Tarigan, File, p. 15; © Stocktrek Images/ SuperStock, p. 16; © Sfocato/Shutterstock.com, p. 17; © ERIK S. LESSER/epa/Corbis, p. 18; © José Antonio Peñas/Science Source, p. 19; © Mark Stouffer Enterprises/Animals Animals, p. 20; © VPC Travel Photo/Alamy, p. 21; © Sandervandijk/Dreamstime.com, p. 22; © Gerry Pearce/Alamy, p. 23; © SmileStudio/Shutterstock.com, p. 24; © kiri y/ Flickr/Getty Images, p. 25; © iStockphoto.com/asiseeit, p. 26; © Sanjay Shrishrimal/ Alamy, p. 27; © iStockphoto.com/yenwen, p. 28; © Donald A Higgs/Photographer's Choice/Getty Images, p. 29; © iStockphoto.com/DaddyBit, p. 30.

Front Cover: © Callan Chesser/Dreamstime.com (top); © Iryna Sosnytska/Dreamstime. com (bottom).

Main body text set in Johann Light 30/36.